Beyond the Moment

Gráinne Hynes with her sister Róisín near their home in Cooke's Point, Cill Chiaráin, Connemara, after Gráinne's First Holy Communion in May 2007

John Carlos FREELANCE

Beyond the Moment

Irish Photojournalism in Our Time

Edited by Colin Jacobson

Introduction by John Banville

The Press Photographers Association of Ireland

The Accidental Art

John Banville

To begin with, an anecdote, probably apocryphal but possibly not. In the days when the *Irish Press* was a going concern and far from gone, a photographer worked there of endearing eccentricity and famously droll humour. One day he was standing in College Green, festooned with the tools of his trade and musing on this and that, when a friend who had been passing by stopped to ask him what he was about. "I'm waiting for an accident to happen," the photographer replied, poker-faced. The friend nodded — "Oh, right" — and they went on chatting for a minute or two. Suddenly, in the roadway in front of them, a car ran into the back of a bus. "Ah," said the friend, preparing to depart, "there's your accident — I'll leave you to it, so."

All art incorporates an element of the contingent. A fleeting play of light and shade across a landscape, a long-lost memory unexpectedly surfacing, a grinding snatch of melody from a barrel organ three streets away — such accidentals will feed into the artist's semi-consciousness and register as tropes long pondered and directed by iron laws. The aleatoric effect is not confined to avant-garde music. There are artists — poets, novelists, paint-pot pourers — who swear by the *I Ching*, the Chinese Book of Changes which claims to divine order in any trail of seemingly chance occurrences. Joyce was dictating a passage of *Finnegans Wake* to his temporary scribe Samuel Beckett when someone knocked on the door; later, when Joyce had the passage read over to him, he wondered at hearing in the middle of it the phrase *Come in!* but, old artificer that he was, he decided to let it stand.

Photography is the swiftest of the art forms, and press photography is swiftest of all. Henri Cartier-Bresson, one of the founders of photojournalism and perhaps its greatest practitioner, has spoken of photography as "fast drawing". For Cartier-Bresson, what he called the "decisive moment" is everything, that instant of almost clairvoyant vision into the heart of a subject, when the artist catches the world *in flagrante*, unaware of how much it is revealing of itself. He was inspired to take up the camera when he saw in a magazine a shot of three naked black youths diving into Lake Tanganyika made by a former sports journalist turned photographer, Martin Munkacsi. Of this picture Cartier-Bresson said: "I suddenly understood that photography can fix eternity in a moment." Shooting a press picture, he wrote, is "recognising an event and at the same instant and within a fraction of a second rigorously organising the forms you see to express and give meaning to the event. It is a matter of putting your brain, your eye and your heart in the same line of sight."

Note that the key terms that Cartier-Bresson employs, "moment", "instant", "fraction of a second", are all divisions of time — "There is only the present," he said to me once, "the present, and eternity" — and time, instantaneous or sempiternal, is the secret inspirer and legislator of photography. How the ancients would envy us our trick of stopping time in the blinking of a shutter; they would think us gods. Heraclitus declared that we never step twice into the same river, but in Frank Miller's wonderful picture of a lost child on the borders between Rwanda and Tanzania during the Rwandan civil war, the river, though in spate, is frozen in time — as is the expression of mingled fear and foreboding on the face of the child standing in a sodden landscape under the useless protection of an umbrella, that perfect symbol of civilised ingenuity.

What are we supposed to feel in face of a press photograph? How far are we to be permitted to admire the artistry of the photographer, and how sternly must we attend to the import of the events being presented graphically to our attention, rather than to the manner of their presentation? What reporter, flying in from a world summit or straggling back at evening from a junior soccer match, would be allowed to begin his report with a long passage of lovingly fashioned landscape painting in prose? What news-editor would tolerate a lyrical description of the precise shade of green of the grass where that child with the umbrella is standing, or of the way the light lends a pewter-glint to the flood-waters, and how the air in the background is blued like the smoke from a gun-barrel . . . ?

Is it the true task of the photojournalist not to make beautiful images but to confront us with the unadorned evidence of "what happened"? The question is moot. Where does art leave off and reporting begin, and vice versa? Should the press photographer aspire to artistry at all, and if not, what is he to do when, rushed by his editor to the scene of some natural or, as often as not, man-made catastrophe, he cannot help producing a series of perfectly composed images of massacre, destruction and human suffering? How can he avoid turning a muddy football game or a military march-past into ballet? The camera never lies, it is said — but ah . . .

One thinks of the printers one worked with in newspapers in the old days, before the arrival of computer setting, who in their youth, during a long and painstaking apprenticeship — and what is art at a certain, fundamental level but a relentless taking of pains? — had been taught the most delicate of skills, from the handmaking of paper to fine bookbinding, and now were condemned to spend their nights ramming inky chunks of hot metal in dull ranks between rules across eight columns. The difference, of course, is that the printers after their apprenticeship was over had no longer any occasion to exercise their skills as mastercraftsmen — perhaps, even, as artists, the best of them — whereas the press photographer, the cameraman, by the nature of his calling, cannot but make beautiful pictures, no matter how terrible or trivial his subject.

Which brings us to the even more moot question as to what, in this context, beauty might consist in. Look at, for instance, Leon Farrell's shot of the anti-globalisation protests on May Day 2004. Can this picture be considered "beautiful"? It was bad in Dublin that day; the gardaí hardly distinguished themselves, and the protestors cannot be said to have done much to further their cause. Farrell's photograph is realistic, it is uncompromising, it is "gritty"; but beautiful? Well, yes. Look, for instance, at the composition of the shot, which Cartier-Bresson might have envied. Those two diagonals made by the water-jets divide the frame into classic proportions, while the force — indeed, the violence — the streaming water represents forms a striking contrast with the curious stillness of the drenched young man posed in the foreground in an attitude of calm defiance. Something in the image transcends the mere recording of a moment; with a few alterations of detail we might be contemplating a scene engraved on the side of a Grecian urn.

Beauty is not the same as prettiness; it is not synonymous with niceness. As Rilke in the *Duino Elegies* assures us,

Beauty's nothing
but beginning of Terror we're still just able to bear . . .

Beauty partakes of the Sublime, whatever distinctions the philosophers may insist on making between the two, and in their way, Farrell's May Day photograph and others similar to it reproduced here *are* beautiful, however grimly so. It is beautiful if for no other reason than that it presents us with a moment of real time caught and emulsified, "fixed", by the alchemist with his camera, a moment that can never come again, and is all the more powerful, all the more affecting, for that very fact: that it is gone.

Another poet, Philip Larkin, a great connoisseur of the evanescent, writes wonderfully of this aspect of photography in a poem entitled, with knowing delicacy, *Lines on a Young Lady's Photograph Album*. Larkin has no illusions about what the camera does —

But o, photography! as no art is,
Faithful and disappointing! that records
Dull days as dull, and hold-it smiles as frauds,
And will not censor blemishes
Like washing-lines, and Hall's-Distemper boards,

But shows the cat as disinclined, and shades
A chin as doubled when it is . . .

— yet recognises with his usual candour and accuracy of expression the power that is conferred on the past, even though it is "a past that no one now can share", by being caught in a photograph:

Those flowers, that gate,
These misty parks and motors, lacerate
Simply by being over . . .

Yes, we are back to time again, or at least to that special case of time which the camera sections off for us.

Photography's subject is the past, and how ironical it is, then, that what the photojournalist is supposedly most concerned with is the present, the stolid here-and-nowness of everyday life. What impresses us when we look through the photographs gathered here, these very emblems of pastness, is the speed with which so many of them must have been taken. All is dash and fleet-of-eye within the static moment caught by the shutter's click. This aspect of the business is illustrated with sly wit in Lorraine O'Sullivan's shot of a cycle race, in which the subject is not so much the race itself as the old man leaning on his bike who looks on with wry amusement as the young racers pedal by in a blur, speeding into their own past. We are reminded that what the photographs in a newspaper often provide is less an illustration of current events than an ironical comment on what is, literally, the passing scene.

And how quickly the present turns to past: look at these faces, these coats and hats and hairstyles; look at the people, anonymous or instantly recognisable, all going, or gone. The rapidity, the merciless rapidity, with which change occurs is one of the — largely unintended — lessons that photography teaches us, and a lesson that press photography teaches most insistently. All the pictures gathered here were of their time, necessarily. That is why they were taken, and what was taken from them was precisely the evidence of the moment. It is really only in after-time that they become what they are, now, for us who view them not in the grey field of a page of newsprint but between the covers of a book. They have gone from being the present of the "decisive moment" to something more lasting, more enduring. It is not eternity — what, *pace* Cartier-Bresson, can human beings know of the eternal other than its name? — but it is not oblivion, either. They have taken on, even the most light-hearted of them, the weight and solemnity of a memorial. Here, they say to us, is something that happened once, had its instant of significance, is past, and will not come again. Despite appearances, the river has flowed on.

Crowds gather to watch Skyfest, part of the annual St Patrick's Festival, at the Custom House, Dublin, in 1999

Joe St Leger
THE IRISH TIMES

Samba dancers join revellers from the nightclub
Spirit in a procession from Temple Bar to the
Middle Abbey Street, Dublin, venue to launch
its fourth-birthday celebrations in May 2006

Crispin Rodwell FREELANCE

Liam O'Doherty and his bride, Fiona
Gilligan, both from Ennis, Co Clare, leave
the Cathedral of Saints Peter and Paul,
Ennis, after their wedding in January 2003

Kenneth O'Halloran FREELANCE

Young Emma Troy looks out the train window on the
West Clare Railway line from Moyasta junction as Private
Gerard Troy and Blainagh Daly share a celebratory
kiss after their wedding at Monmore church in 2001

John C Kelly THE CLARE CHAMPION

Mary Murphy, accompanied by her father, Noel
Murphy, casts her General Election vote at St
Mark's School, Tallaght, Co Dublin immediately
before her marriage to Pat McDonald in June 1997

Alan Betson THE IRISH TIMES

Greg and Tina Downey from California, USA,
have their marriage blessed by the Church
of Ire and rector Reverend Bob Hanna at the
Cliffs of Moher, Co Clare, in spring 1998

Eamon Ward THE CLARE CHAMPION

Pedestrians in Galway city centre
take shelter under a shop canopy
during a cloudburst in July 2007

Joe O'Shaughnessy
THE CONNACHT TRIBUNE

Members of Our Lady's Choral
Society brave a hail shower in
April 1999 on the occasion of
their annual performance of
Handel's *Messiah* at Fishamble
Street, Dublin, where, in 1742,
the music was first performed

Pat Langan THE IRISH TIMES

Townsfolk get ferried to dry ground in the bucket of a digger after the river Suir burst its banks by the Old Bridge in Clonmel in October 2004

Brenda Fitzsimons
THE IRISH TIMES

A pedestrian steps into a patch of light as rain and wind lash Dublin's O'Connell Bridge in November 2003

Gary Ashe
ALLPIX / IRISH DAILY STAR

The Taoiseach Bertie Ahern surveys
the floods after the river Tolka burst its
banks in his Drumcondra, Dublin,
constituency in mid-November 2002

Colin Keegan COLLINS PHOTO AGENCY

Jack Mulveen feeds the birds at the Claddagh, Galway city, after a fall of snow in December 2000

Joe O'Shaughnessy
THE CONNACHT TRIBUNE

Swimmers brave the icy water during a snowfall
at Blackrock, Galway, in December 2004

Joe O'Shaughnessy THE CONNACHT TRIBUNE

Competitors take the plunge near Dublin's Rory O'More bridge at the start of the 85th annual Liffey Swim in September 2005

Fran Veale FREELANCE

Competitors shower on the quayside after the Liffey Swim in August 1996

Frank Miller
THE IRISH TIMES

Young swimmers wait for their race during
the National Community Games finals
at Mosney, Co Meath, in August 2000

Brenda Fitzsimons THE IRISH TIMES

The Christmas Day swim at the Forty
Foot, Sandycove, Dublin Bay, in 2003

Julien Behal MAXWELL PHOTOGRAPHY

Swimmers take the plunge
from the Blackrock diving
tower in Galway during
hot weather in May 2008

Joe O'Shaughnessy
THE CONNACHT TRIBUNE

The Dublin Fish Market in
St Michan's Street shortly
before its closure for the last
time in April 2005

Lar Boland FREELANCE

Dublin's oldest street market, The Hill, at Cumberland Street North, in 1998. It is also known to locals as The Stones, because goods for sale are laid out on the cobbles

Lar Boland FREELANCE

The Great October Horse Fair at
Ballinasloe, Co Galway, in 1995

Joe St Leger THE IRISH TIMES

Children and their horse enjoy
the August sunshine during Puck
Fair, Killorglin, Co Kerry, in 2005

Eamon Ward FREELANCE

A man and his horse head home
from the Great October Horse
Fair in Ballinasloe in 2006

Eamon Ward
FREELANCE / THE CLARE PEOPLE

The folklorist Dr Éamon
Lankford at work on Cape
Clear Island, Co Cork, in 2003
during a research project on
place-names in Cork and Kerry

Frank Miller THE IRISH TIMES

A crow faces into a blizzard at Ballinstockan,
near Blessington, Co Wicklow, in winter 2001

Colman Doyle

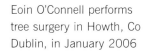

Eoin O'Connell performs
tree surgery in Howth, Co
Dublin, in January 2006

Mark Condren

A sign at the site of a planned housing development near Kilcock, Co Kildare, in April 2006, indicates the market's vibrancy during the property boom

Kenneth O'Halloran FREELANCE

Leftover sandwiches at the launch in March 2006 of the Tallow and the Waxworks, residential buildings for sale at Ashtown, Co Dublin

Kenneth O'Halloran FREELANCE

A microphone stands ready for the visit by the Taoiseach
Bertie Ahern to Cornafulla National School, Athlone,
during the General Election campaign of May 2007

Kenneth O'Halloran FREELANCE

A woman basks in the sun at Palmers Rock, Salthill, Galway, in May, 2004

Joe O'Shaughnessy
THE CONNACHT TRIBUNE

An armed detective guards the house in Farran, Co Cork, where an estimated £5 million sterling was found in February 2005. The cash was believed to be from the December 2004 Northern Bank robbery in Belfast

Daragh McSweeney PROVISION

The blood-flecked feet of the drug dealer David Weafer protrude from the doorway of his Finglas home after he had been shot in the head in a gangland murder in June 1995

Steve Humphreys
IRISH INDEPENDENT

The body of three-month-old Leilah Hickey, stabbed to death in April 2000, is taken from her home in Newbridge, Co Kildare. Her father, Derek Hickey, would later plead guilty to the murder

Brenda Fitzsimons
THE IRISH TIMES

The paedophile priest Brendan Smyth is
led from the Four Courts in Dublin after
being sentenced to 12 years in July 1997

Steve Humphreys IRISH INDEPENDENT

Anthony Butler leaves Dublin's Four
Courts in May 1997 to start a life
sentence after his conviction for the
murder of Sandra Tobin in her home at
Closegate, Waterford, the previous year

Alan Betson THE IRISH TIMES

Patrice Harrington waves the Irish
Tricolour in protest on the Great Blasket
during a legal dispute over landing rights
on the West Kerry island in July 2006

Domnick Walsh EYE FOCUS

Orangemen face police and soldiers through barbed wire at Drumcree Church on the fourth day of a stand-off over the government's refusal to allow a parade through the Catholic Garvaghy Road, Portadown, in July 1998

Crispin Rodwell FREELANCE

Dr Ian Paisley, leader of Northern Ireland's Democratic Unionist Party, during peace-agreement talks at Stormont in 1998

Alan Betson THE IRISH TIMES

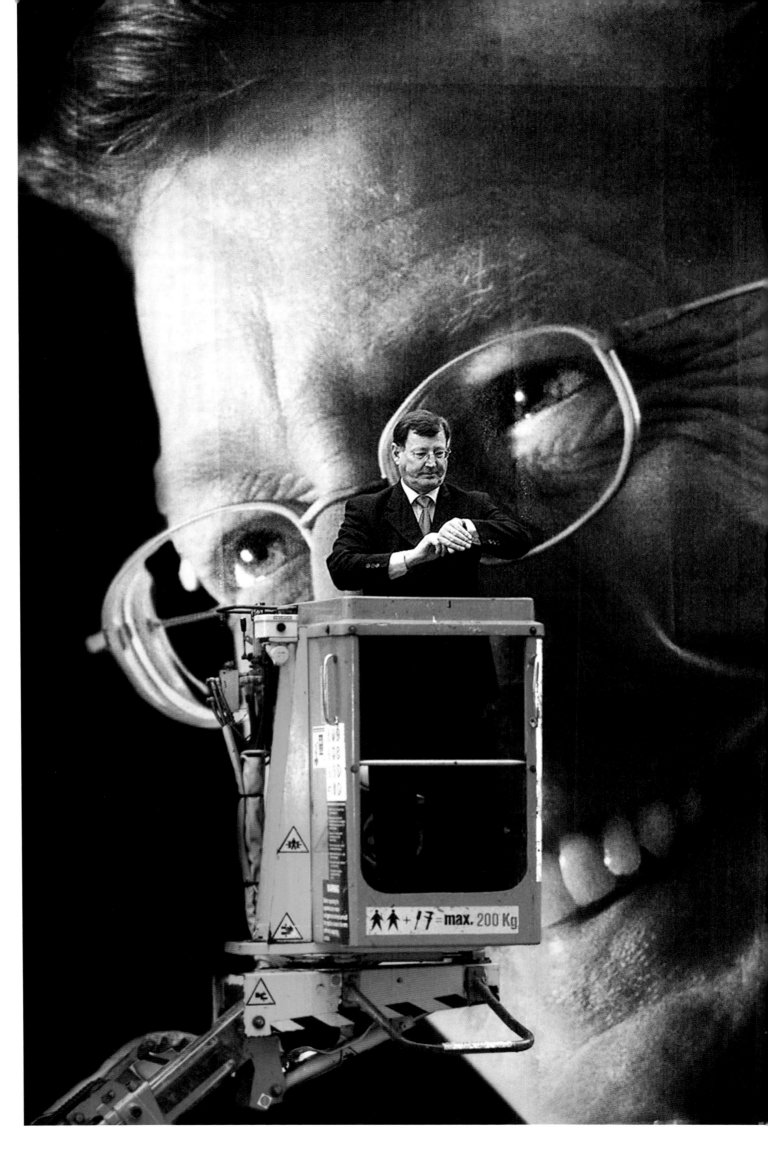

The Ulster Unionist leader David Trimble launches his hoarding campaign in Glengall St, Belfast, in March 2001 ahead of the Westminster elections

Ann McManus THE IRISH NEWS

Ian Paisley, as First Minister, delivers the historic 'Devolution Day' speech at Stormont to mark the restoration on 8 May 2007 of parliamentary structures in Northern Ireland after decades of conflict and direct rule from Westminster

John Harrison HARRISON PHOTOGRAPHY

The former Taoiseach Charles Haughey
and his son Seán canvass for votes
in Dublin North Central ahead of the
November 1992 General Election

Paddy Whelan THE IRISH TIMES

The Taoiseach Bertie Ahern
hugs a supporter in Carlow town
during his nationwide General
Election tour in May 2007

Eamonn Farrell
PHOTOCALL IRELAND

The US ambassador to Ireland
James Kenny meets his cousin
Derek Kenny during a visit to
the ancestral home in Killasser,
Co Mayo, in September 2005

Henry Wills
WESTERN PEOPLE

The Green Party chairman, John Gormley (left), confronts the leader of the Progressive Democrats, Michael McDowell, on the hustings in Ranelagh, Dublin, in May 2007. Gormley was contesting the PD claim that a Green Party in government would increase corporation tax

Frank Miller THE IRISH TIMES

Michael Noonan, leader of the Fine
Gael party, surprises a voter and
his dogs on the campaign trail in
Naas, Co Kildare, in April 2002

Brenda Fitzsimons
THE IRISH TIMES

Joe Costello of the Labour
Party is hoisted by supporters
celebrating his re-election to Dáil
Éireann at the vote count in
the RDS, Dublin, in May 2002

Marc O'Sullivan
COLLINS PHOTO AGENCY

Garda Jim Brennan; David Alcorn, the presiding
officer; and Donal Ó Dufaigh, a radio reporter,
return from Inishfree Island to Burtonport,
Co Donegal, with the General Election ballot box,
containing two votes, in November 1992

Frank Miller THE IRISH TIMES

The former Taoiseach and Fianna
Fáil leader Charles Haughey, having
relinquished his seat, stands at
a window of Leinster House on the
day the newly elected 27th Dáil
convened in December 1992

Leon Farrel PHOTOCALL IRELAND

Well-wishers turn out in Tullamore, Co
Offaly, to welcome Brian Cowen home after
his election as Taoiseach in May 2008

Bryan O'Brien THE IRISH TIMES

The Taoiseach Bertie Ahern crosses
the cobblestones in front of
Government Buildings shortly after
announcing in April 2008 his
intention to relinquish leadership of
the country and the Fianna Fáil party

Christopher Doyle THE IRISH SUN

The Minister for Education and Science Mary Hanafin peers through an antique telescope at the official reopening of the Crawford Observatory at University College Cork in June 2006

Daragh McSweeney

The Labour Party leader Pat Rabbitte, on a visit
to Mary Mother of Hope National School, Clonee,
Co Meath, in May 2007, samples a cake
provided by the school to mark his 58th birthday

Julien Behal THE PRESS ASSOCIATION OF IRELAND

Clara Salinger, Clifford Walron, Neil Quinlan and Johnny Duff of St Oliver
Plunkett's School, Monkstown, Co Dublin, perform a welcoming ceremony
in April 2004 for countries newly admitted to the European Union

Frank Miller THE IRISH TIMES

Children from Dublin's Hedley Park school
release balloons on Grafton Street in June
2007 to mark the 50th day since the
disappearance in Portugal of the four-
year-old English girl Madeleine McCann

David Sleator THE IRISH TIMES

President Mary McAleese and Ethan Wilson sit in the garden at the official opening in May 2004 of St Vincent's Centre, for children with intellectual disabilities, on Dublin's Navan Road

Jim O'Kelly IRISH INDEPENDENT

The Minister for Defence Willie
O'Dea stands for the National
Anthem during the commissioning
of cadets at the Curragh Military
Camp, Co Kildare, in January 2007

Julien Behal
THE PRESS ASSOCIATION OF IRELAND

The US president George W Bush and the
Taoiseach Bertie Ahern step it out in the grounds
of Dromoland Castle, Co Clare, in June 2004

Mark Maxwell MAXWELL PHOTOGRAPHY

The US president Bill Clinton, in Ireland on a book-signing tour, meets Joan Fitzgerald Quinn (83), Mary Quinn (84) and Peggy Wallace (80), all of Sutton Golf Club, before teeing off at Royal Dublin Golf Club in August 2004

Steve Humphreys IRISH INDEPENDENT

The US president Bill Clinton addresses a crowd in the Border town of Dundalk, Co Louth, before going on to Belfast for peace-process meetings in November 2000

Bryan O'Brien THE IRISH TIMES

The Sinn Féin leader Gerry Adams and his party
colleague Mary Lou McDonald at their party's Árd
Chomhairle (national executive meeting) in Sinn Féin's
offices, Parnell Square, Dublin, in January 2006

Bryan O'Brien THE IRISH TIMES

The Taoiseach Bertie Ahern takes a
phone call in his car after turning
the sod for a new library at Dublin
City University in January 1999

Matt Kavanagh THE IRISH TIMES

Stormont security officials prevent the convicted loyalist
killer Michael Stone from entering Parliament Buildings,
Belfast, where in November 2006 a meeting was
being held to select ministers for the new Assembly

Peter Morrison ASSOCIATED PRESS

The Sinn Féin president Gerry Adams retaliates after a snowball ambush by youths during the local-election campaign in Trim, Co Meath, in February 2005

Matt Kavanagh THE IRISH TIMES

President Mary Robinson is greeted by an
admirer on arrival in June 1993 to launch the
Ballymun Partnership, an organisation
dedicated to creating jobs in the Dublin suburb

Mick Slevin IRISH PRESS GROUP

A man lies pinned under a car after a
road accident in Limerick city in 1993

Garrett Hurley PRESS 22

An RUC officer shoots his pistol in the air to save an ambushed colleague during a disturbance in Derry in 1998

Martin McCullough
FREELANCE

A mob attacks a British Army land rover
in the Ardoyne, north Belfast, in 2002

Brendan Murphy THE IRISH NEWS

The devastated commercial centre of
Coleraine, Co Derry smoulders at first light
on 14 November 1992 after the detonation
of a 500lb IRA van bomb the night before

Peter Nash FREELANCE

A Catholic child on her way to Holy Cross Primary School, north Belfast, clings to her mother as they run the gauntlet of loyalist demonstrators in June 2001

William Cherry PACEMAKER PRESS

A boy at a bonfire in east Belfast
makes a pointed gesture on the eve
of the annual Protestant celebration
of the 12th of July in 2000

Bryan O'Brien THE IRISH TIMES

A Protestant youth watches the traditional '11th night' bonfire on Belfast's Shankill Road in July 2007

Niall Carson
THE PRESS ASSOCIATION OF IRELAND

British Army land rovers burn during loyalist
rioting in west Belfast following the rerouting of
an Orange Order march in September 2005

Crispin Rodwell FREELANCE

A garda stands by a burning car in Dublin's Nassau Street during riots following the Love Ulster march in February 2006

Tony Gavin SUNDAY INDEPENDENT

A young man defies a Garda water
cannon during clashes between May Day
protestors and gardaí on the Navan Road
beside Dublin's Phoenix Park in 2004

Leon Farrell PHOTOCALL IRELAND

Gardaí arrest a man as members of the Traveller community protest at the closing of Dunsink Lane, Co Dublin, blocking direct access to Finglas village from their encampment, in October 2004

Colin Keegan COLLINS PHOTO AGENCY

The US diplomat Henry Kissinger enters University College Cork to address a business conference, in February 2002, heavily guarded as protestors voice disapproval of his views and political record

Donna McBride PROVISION

Eleven months after the murder in January 2006 of the 38-year-old mother-of-one Siobhan Kearney, her sisters hold a vigil outside her Goatstown, Co Dublin, home, where her body was found. Siobhan's husband, Brian, was sentenced in March 2008 to life for the murder

Bryan O'Brien THE IRISH TIMES

Paul Abayomi, wearing a blood-stained jacket following an assault in Dublin city, joins with other asylum seekers in an anti-racism demonstration on O'Connell Street in April 2000

Frank Miller THE IRISH TIMES

Supporters and opponents demonstrate outside Belfast City Hall, where Ireland's first 'gay marriage' was taking place, in December 2005

Brendan Murphy

THE IRISH NEWS

Anne Katrin Linde (forefront with black
mask) from Bandon, Co Cork, with
members of the National Youth Council
at a HIV/AIDS awareness ceremony in
Dublin Castle in November 2006

Steve Humphreys IRISH INDEPENDENT

Opponents of abortion take
part in a Youth Defence
procession on Dublin's O'Connell
Street in March 1995

John Carlos THE SUNDAY TRIBUNE

Angel Serrano of Talavera de la Reina, Spain, shortly before his death at the age of 56 from Alzheimer's in October 2004, is cared for and comforted day and night by his wife, Dioni, youngest son, Carlos, and daughter Christina. He had been suffering from the disease for 10 years

Kenneth O'Halloran FREELANCE

An evicted woman stands among
the goods and chattels left outside
her flat by the city sheriff in
Dublin's North Inner City in 1998

Eric Luke THE IRISH TIMES

Nora Mongans and her son Jason peer out of the tent in which they and Jason's seven siblings slept when their caravan was destroyed by fire at Lahinch, Co Clare, in November 2003

Eamon Ward THE CLARE CHAMPION

A gypsy woman camped illegally on the
M50 roundabout in Ballymun, Dublin,
with about 200 other Roma, shortly
before their deportation following an
early-morning Garda raid in July 2007

Julien Behal
THE PRESS ASSOCIATION OF IRELAND

A displaced child cn a
hillside having crossed the
Kagera River into Tanzania
during the civil war that
followed the genocide in
Rwanda in May 1994

Frank Miller
THE IRISH TIMES

Mourners at the Dublin
Mosque, Clonskeagh, with the
coffins of Eman Ayadi and Aya
Chenniti, who were killed in a
traffic accident in March 2008

Garry O'Neill FREELANCE

Jamie Farrelly Maughan's sister Rebecca and mother,
Josephine Farrelly, at Jamie's funeral in Cavan town
in July 2004.The body of the 13-year-old had been
found in the garden of a vacant house yards from
her mother's home six days after her disappearance

Mark Condren THE SUNDAY TRIBUNE

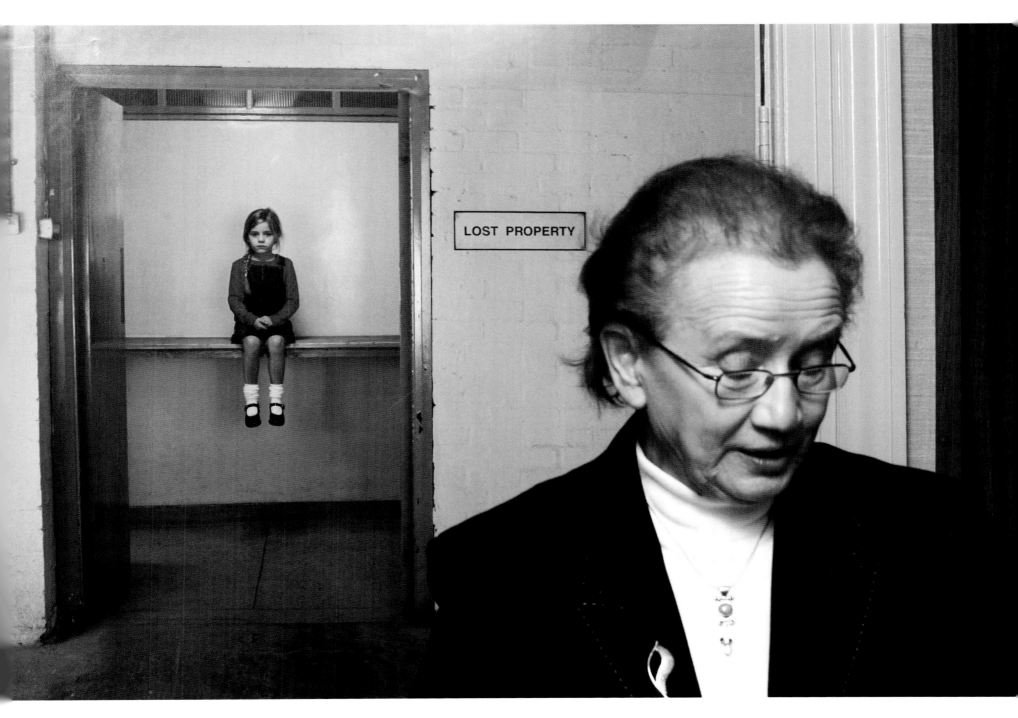

The former Supreme Court judge Catherine McGuinness speaks in February 2007 at the launch in Dublin of a campaign by the charity Barnardos for constitutional guarantees of children's rights

Frank Miller THE IRISH TIMES

Facing page: a young woman sleeps
on the floor in the early hours after
the annual Trinity Ball in Dublin;
above: passers-by await the arrival of
an ambulance for a man collapsed in
Temple Bar, Dublin's popular nightlife
sector; right: a man and a woman in
each other's arms in a Co Clare bar long
after midnight during the Lisdoonvarna
Matchmaking Festival — all in 2006

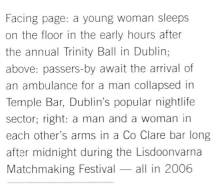

Kenneth O'Halloran FREELANCE

105

Dublin 2006 — above: a man is treated in an ambulance after a drink-related assault as revellers pour onto the streets with the 4am closing of nightclubs; left: two young women in nurses' uniforms in Temple Bar after a hen night; facing page: a young woman in a fairy outfit tries to wave down a taxi at 4am in the city centre

Kenneth O'Halloran FREELANCE

A man and woman escape the
February chill in the Simon
Community's emergency night shelter
in Harcourt Street, Dublin, in 2004

Fran Veale FREELANCE

Michael O'Boyle, a Co Leitrim
bachelor, watches television amid
the clutter of his one-room flat in
Manorhamilton in July 2005

Mark Condren THE SUNDAY TRIBUNE

Patrick Dwyer of Laharn,
Castlemaine, Co Kerry, prepares
the pet turkey destined for the
family table at Christmas 2006

Domnick Walsh EYE FOCUS

A bull breaks out of its pen at
an agricultural show in Bantry,
Co Cork, in September 2005

Des Barry IRISH EXAMINER

Ireland's first elected mayor from the Traveller
community, Tuam's Martin Ward, wears his chain
of office while visiting constituents in 2003

Ray Ryan THE TUAM HERALD

The father and two brothers of a bride to be
pass the time in the O'Reillys' kitchen in
Clonmel on the day of the wedding in 2003

John D Kelly FREELANCE / THE NATIONALIST

A boy of the Traveller community
wears his Sunday suit at Tallow
horse fair, Co Cork, in 2000

Kenneth O'Halloran FREELANCE

A woman waits for a bus in West
Tallaght, Co Dublin, in 1996

Kate Horgan FREELANCE

A man drinks water from a
holy well at Glencolmcille,
Co Donegal, in 1998

Lar Boland FREELANCE

Michael and Matthew O'Halloran, who run a
family undertakers in Corofin, Co Clare, prepare
for a funeral in June 2002 while Matthew's
wife, Eileen, hangs out the washing

Kenneth O'Halloran FREELANCE

Robert Walsh, Máiréad Horan, Margaret Hayes and Mary Kiely, Leaving Cert students from Dromcollogher Community College, Co Cork, enact a wake in class in January 2000

Brian Gavin PRESS 22

The writer Francis Stuart, laid
out at his home in Fanore,
Co Clare, after his death at the
age of 97 in February 2000

Eric Luke THE IRISH TIMES

Mourners file past the grave of the former
international footballer George Best following
the funeral in Belfast in December 2005

Kenneth O'Halloran FREELANCE

A fan carries five red roses and a picture of George Best during the funeral at Stormont, Belfast, in December 2005

Cyril Byrne THE IRISH TIMES

A year on from the destruction of the World Trade Centre in New York in September 2001, Margaret McHugh, who lost her daughter Anne Marie in the attacks, attends a memorial ceremony in Dublin

Bryan O'Brien
THE IRISH TIMES

The remains of the former Taoiseach Charles Haughey pass along the Clontarf seafront en route to St Fintan's cemetery, Sutton, Co Dublin, in June 2006

David Conachy SUNDAY INDEPENDENT

The Taoiseach Bertie Ahern with Mrs Maureen Haughey, her sons Conor (left) and Ciarán (right) and Conor's son Cathal at the funeral of Charles Haughey in Sutton in June 2006

Eric Luke THE IRISH TIMES

The body of Mother Teresa arrives for burial at the mother house of the Missionaries cf Charity, Calcutta, in September 1997

Eric Luke THE IRISH TIMES

A resident of Banda Aceh, Sumatra, reclaims belongings from the ruins of her home after the Indian Ocean earthquake and tsunami of December 2004 that killed tens of thousands and devastated coastal communities

Kenneth O'Halloran FREELANCE

Adi Roche, director of the Chernobyl
Children's Project, crosses a
radioactive bridge over the river
Dnieper, with the Chernobyl reactor
in the background, in 2004

Julien Behal FREELANCE

Employees of the computer-chip manufacturer Intel perform stretching exercises during work in the 'clean room' of the Leixlip, Co Kildare, plant in December 1999

Frank Miller THE IRISH TIMES

Special Apostle A Ooladukun baptises
a member of the Eternal Sacred Order
of Cherubim & Seraphim Church
of Noah's Ark at Ennis swimming
pool, Co Clare, in May 2002

John C Kelly THE CLARE CHAMPION

Pupils of Killaghtee National School, Co Donegal, walk to the church to rehearse for their school's Nativity play in December 2001

Brenda Fitzsimons THE IRISH TIMES

A boy wearing the Galway jersey pays his respects to the football legend Seán Purcell during the reposal at St Jarlath's College, Tuam, in August 2005

Joe O'Shaughnessy
THE CONNACHT TRIBUNE

Nuns of the enclosed order of
Poor Clare in Ennis, Co Clare,
watch the funeral of Pope John
Paul II on television in April 2005

Eamon Ward FREELANCE

Cardinal Desmond Connell
dresses for a Mass in St Mary's
Pro-Cathedral, Dublin, to mark the
50th anniversary, in May 2001,
of his ordination to the priesthood

Moya Nolan

FREELANCE / THE IRISH TIMES

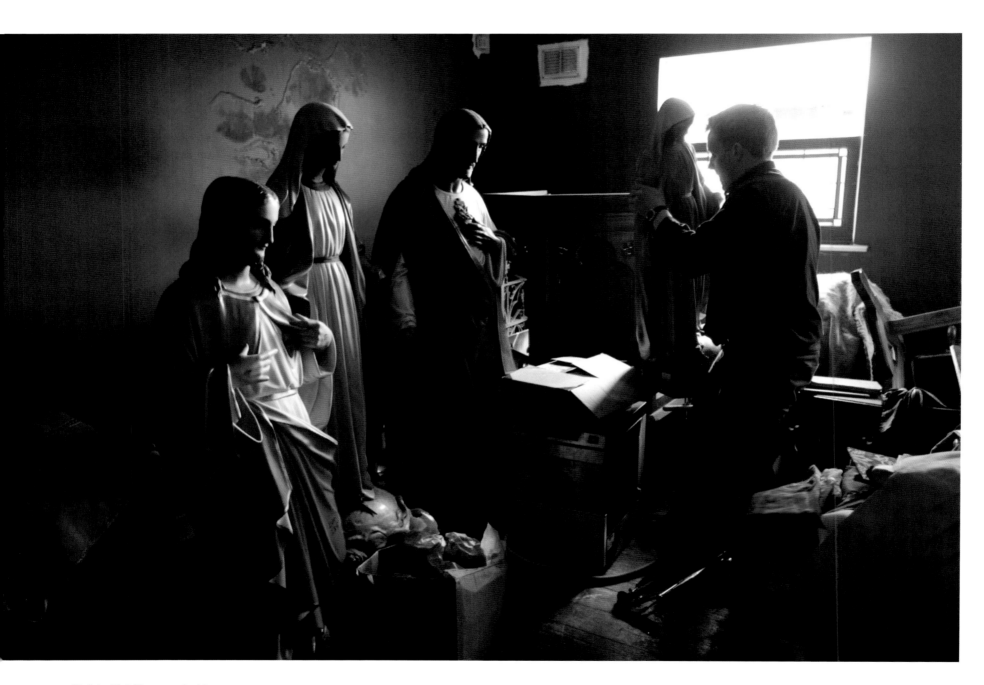

Christy Bird Flanagan in his
furniture and antiques shop,
Christy Bird's, at Portobello
Bridge, Dublin, in May 2005

Bryan O'Brien THE IRISH TIMES

A woman kisses the relics of Saint Anthony of Padua in the Church of the Immaculate Conception (Adam & Eve's), Merchant's Quay, Dublin, during the relics' tour of Ireland in 2003

Aidan Crawley FREELANCE

Pilgrims climb Croagh Patrick, Co Mayo, on 'Reek Sunday', 2005. The annual pilgrimage on the last Sunday in July commemorates St Patrick's 40-day fast on the mountain in AD 441 and attracts tens of thousands. Mass is celebrated and confessions are heard in a small chapel on the 2,510-foot summit

Kenneth O'Halloran
FREELANCE

Two elderly pilgrims help each other while
climbing a mist-enshrouded Croagh Patrick,
Co Mayo, on Reek Sunday, July 2001

Joe St Leger THE IRISH TIMES

Pilgrims carry a 24-foot cross up
Knockshee mountain, Co Down,
on Good Friday, April 1993

Frank Miller THE IRISH TIMES

Pilgrims perform barefoot rounds
of the Penitential Beds at Lough
Derg, Co Donegal, in 2004

Eamon Ward FREELANCE

A pilgrim takes part in three days
of prayer, penance and self-denial
at St Patrick's Purgatorial Island,
Lough Derg, Co Donegal, in 2004

Eamon Ward FREELANCE

John Healy from Kilnamattra, Macroom, Co Cork,
and Margaret Lucey from Inchigeela, Co Cork,
complete the May Day rounds at the 'City of Shrone'
pilgrimage site, Rathmore, Co Kerry, in 2006

Valerie O'Sullivan FREELANCE

A woman makes the May Day 2006 rounds at the 'City of Shrone', Rathmore, Co Kerry, said to be the oldest pilgrimage site in Western Europe

Valerie O'Sullivan FREELANCE

The Lismorahaun Singers
perform during the annual
Burren Ramble in Poul Barron,
near Fanore, Co Clare, in 2006

John C Kelly
THE CLARE CHAMPION

Spectators by the 15th green on the first day of golf's Ryder Cup, between
Europe and the USA, at The K Club, Co Kildare, in September 2006

Alan Betson THE IRISH TIMES

Visitors shelter from a
downpour during the first in a
series of open days at
Farmleigh House, in Dublin's
Phoenix Park, in July 2004

Alan Betson THE IRISH TIMES

Strange Fruit, an Australian festival
and theatre company, perform at the
Galway Arts Festival in July 2004

Joe O'Shaughnessy
THE CONNACHT TRIBUNE

The eco artist Gerard Dowling in
his Middle Abbey Street, Dublin,
dwelling in August 2007 with
a work made from traffic cones
salvaged from the river Liffey

Julien Behal
THE PRESS ASSOCIATION OF IRELAND

The sculptor Ian Stuart, son of the writer
Francis Stuart, in his conservatory at
Laragh, Co Wicklow, in March 2007

Tony Gavin SUNDAY INDEPENDENT

Tibetan monks on a visit to Dublin's Chester
Beatty Library in November 2000 create a
Buddhist sand mandala destined upon
completion for ritual dispersal on the river Liffey

Lar Boland FREELANCE

A parking meter
covered with graffiti on
Dublin's Windmill Lane
merges with the wall
behind in July 2007

Dennis Scannell
IRISH EXAMINER

A dancer performs in the Outre variety
show, part of the Fringe Theatre
Festival, in the Spiegeltent at Dublin
Docklands in September 2007

Julien Behal
THE PRESS ASSOCIATION OF IRELAND

Visitors walk through the
Luminarium, one of the St Patrick's
Festival attractions, in Dublin's
Merrion Square in March 2004

David Sleator THE IRISH TIMES

The artist Kordula Packard at work with
an attentive companion on Sherkin
Island, West Cork, in February 2005

Daragh McSweeney PROVISION

The artist Camille Souter during
a quiet moment at her home on
Achill Island in March 2001

Brenda Fitzsimons
THE IRISH TIMES

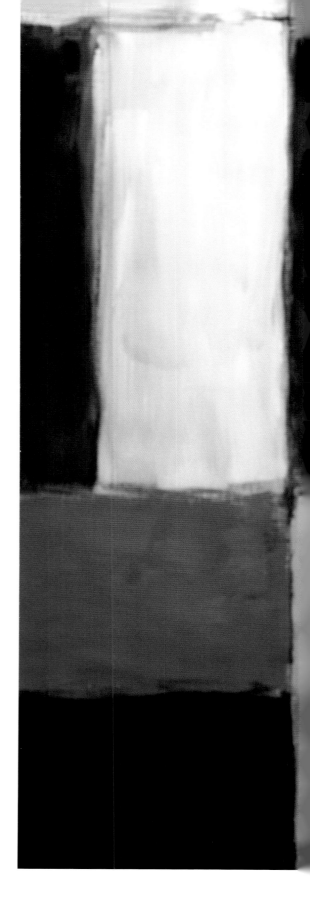

A member of the Stanislavsky
Theatre Ballet from Moscow
takes a smoking break at
the Point Theatre, Dublin in
December 1999

Lar Boland FREELANCE

The model Yomiko Chen poses before a painting in the Sean Scully room of the Hugh Lane Gallery in Dublin's Parnell Square in April 2006

Bryan O'Brien THE IRISH TIMES

Performers mourn the 'loss of green spaces'
during the Carnival Parade called Morning,
Noon and Night for the cultural festival Project
06 in Galway city in July 2006

Joe O'Shaughnessy THE CONNACHT TRIBUNE

Dancers Jessica Edgley, Larissa Law, Melanie
Perks and Rachel Horn rehearse *Bamboo Spring*
ahead of the ballet's premiere at the Mermaid
Arts Centre, Bray, Co Wicklow, in April 2004

Steve Humphreys IRISH INDEPENDENT

Players of the Druid Theatre perform
John B Keane's *Sive* at the Gleneagle
hotel, Killarney, in April 2003

Valerie O'Sullivan FREELANCE

Members of the street-theatre
group Macnas perform
during the Halloween parade
in Galway city in 2004

Joe O'Shaughnessy
THE CONNACHT TRIBUNE

The Minister for Arts, Culture and the Gaeltacht, Michael D Higgins, at the Town Hall Theatre, Galway, to announce details of Baboró, an international arts festival for children, in April 1997

Joe O'Shaughnessy
THE CONNACHT TRIBUNE

Members of the Russian
Theatre group Derevo
perform during the opening
of the Dublin Fringe
Festival at George's Dock
in September 2007

Cyril Byrne
THE IRISH TIMES

Katie Jones (four), Orla Burns
(five) and Bronagh Kelly (four)
at the children's Christmas ballet
in the University Concert Hall,
Limerick, in December 2004

Marie McCallan PRESS 22

A young boy is given an aerial view
during a concert at the Mitchelstown
Music Festival, Co Cork, in August 2000

John D Kelly FREELANCE / THE NATIONALIST

Johnny Cash and Kris Kristofferson perform at the University Concert Hall, Limerick, in February 1993

Eamon Ward FREELANCE

Michael Jackson performs at the RDS, Dublin, during the HIStory World Tour in June 1997

Steve Humphreys
IRISH INDEPENDENT

Bono and Adam Clayton of U2 on stage
at Lansdowne Road, Dublin, during
the Pop Mart world tour in August 1997

Steve Humphreys IRISH INDEPENDENT

Mick Jagger on stage with
the Rolling Stones at The Point,
Dublin, in September 2003

Tony Gavin
SUNDAY INDEPENDENT

A busker plays saxophone in Lombard
Street, Belfast, in June 2006

Brendan Murphy THE IRISH NEWS

The singer Shane MacGowan at North
Lotts, Dublin city, in November 2004

David Conachy SUNDAY INDEPENDENT

The Belgian musician Toots
Thielemans plays harmonica at the
Cork Jazz Festival in October 2000

Matt Kavanagh THE IRISH TIMES

The singer Shane MacGowan
poses for a portrait in Nenagh,
Co Tipperary, in 2004

Pádraig Ó Flannabhra
FREELANCE

The English theatre director, television presenter and medical doctor Jonathan Miller at the Gate Theatre, Dublin, to direct William Congreve's *The Double Dealer* in November 1992

John Carlos THE SUNDAY TRIBUNE

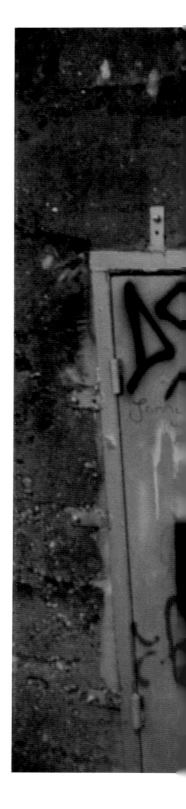

The singer Sinéad
O'Connor at an anti-war
demonstration on
O'Connell Street, Dublin,
in March 1993

Darren Kinsella
FREELANCE

The Galway-born crime
writer Ken Bruen at Woodquay
in the city in April 2003

Joe O'Shaughnessy
THE CONNACHT TRIBUNE

The novelist William Trevor at the unveiling of a bronze
sculpture in his honour in the main square of his
home town, Mitchelstown, Co Cork, in August 2004

Daragh McSweeney PROVISION

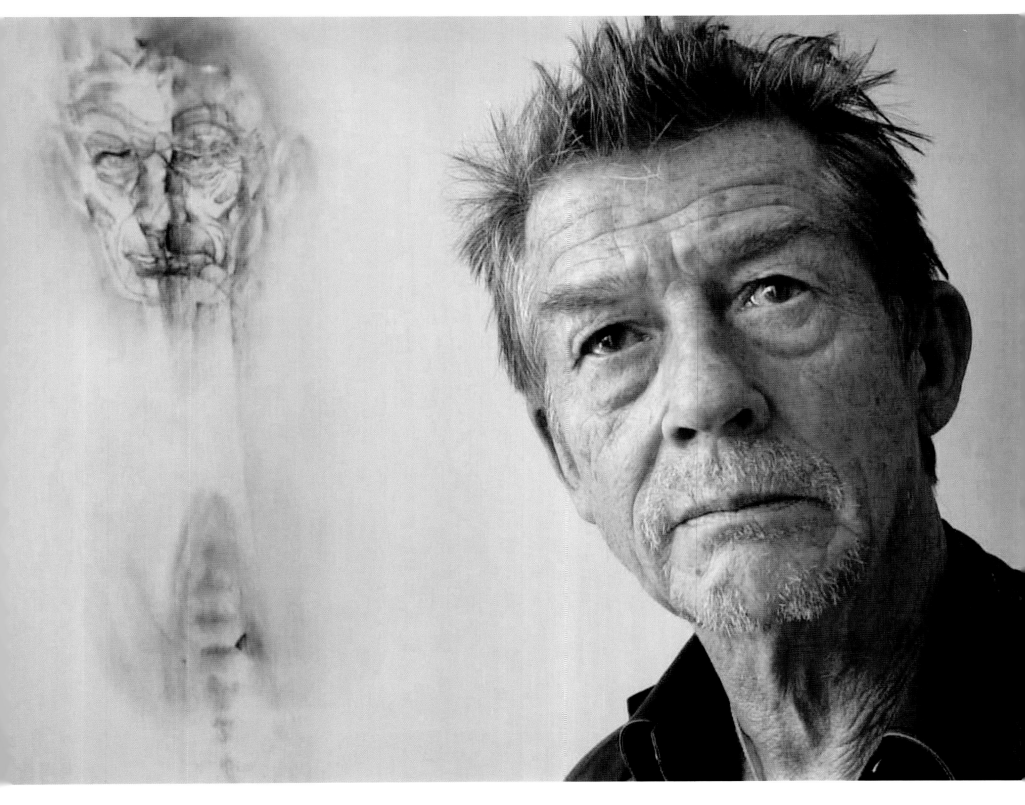

The actor John Hurt at Dublin's
Gate Theatre in August 2001

Joe St Leger THE IRISH TIMES

Professor Michael Porter
speaks on business
strategy at the IMI
conference centre in
Dublin in October 2003

Frank Miller
THE IRISH TIMES

Clonycavan Man, the Iron
Age body found in a bog in
Co Meath in 2003, after
preservation work at the National
Museum of Ireland, Collins
Barracks, Dublin, in January 2006

Frank Miller THE IRISH TIMES

Children in the kitchen of their home in the
economically depressed Belarus of 2005

Ray Ryan THE TUAM HERALD

Paulina Orlikowska from
Poland sheds a tear on her first
day attending the Presentation
Primary School, Clonmel, Co
Tipperary, in September 2005

John D Kelly
FREELANCE / THE NATIONALIST

A Russian clown waits
to take the stage at Dublin's
Gaiety Theatre in 1998

Lar Boland FREELANCE

Two children — one wearing an old Russian army uniform — in Vesnova orphanage, Belarus, in 2004

Julien Behal SUNDAY INDEPENDENT

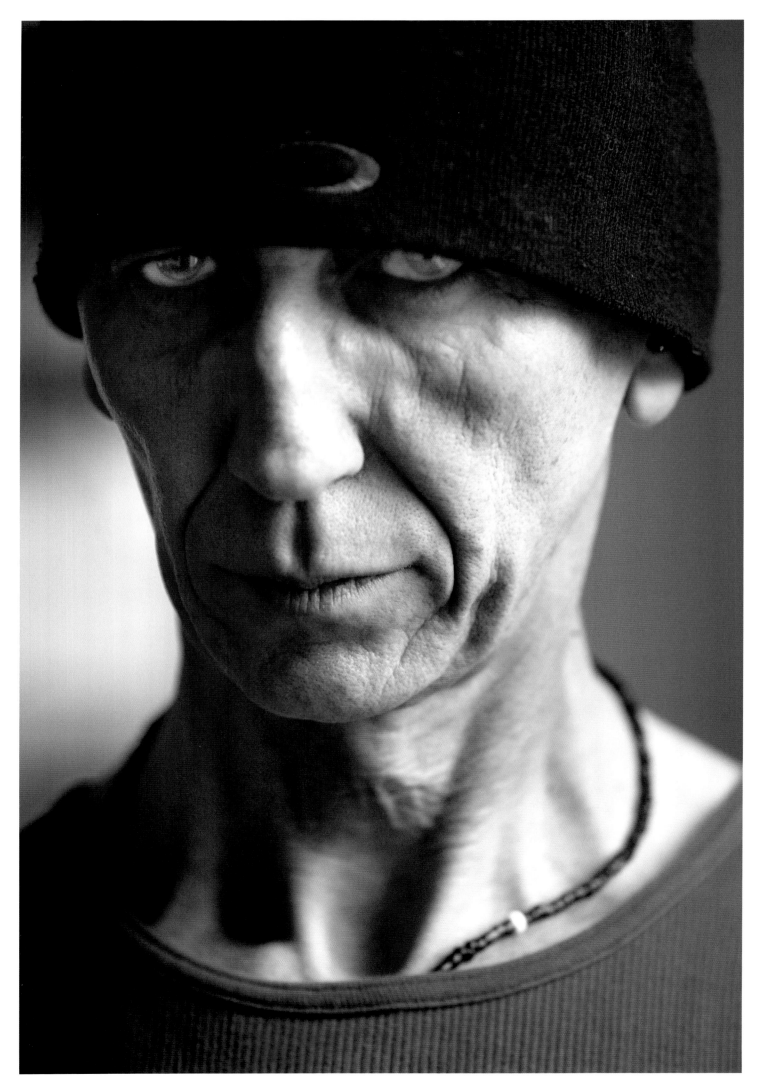

The artist Charlie Whisker
in January 2007

Tony Gavin
SUNDAY INDEPENDENT

The actor-director Peter Kennedy prepares
for his role in an Ennis Musical Society
production of *The Inmate* in 2000

John C Kelly THE CLARE CHAMPION

The actor Richard Harris at Dunlicky,
Co Clare, in July 2001 during the
making of a documentary about his life

Brian Gavin PRESS 22

Brother Columbanus Deegan on Tramore strand, Co Waterford, in June 2004 on the eve of his return to Normandy for the 50th anniversary commemoration of the invasion. The D-Day veteran holds a photograph of himself as an RAF airman

Frank Miller THE IRISH TIMES

Bob Doyle in February 2007, when he
had become the last surviving Irishman
to have fought on the Republican side
in the Spanish Civil War

Cillian Kelly NEWS DIGITAL

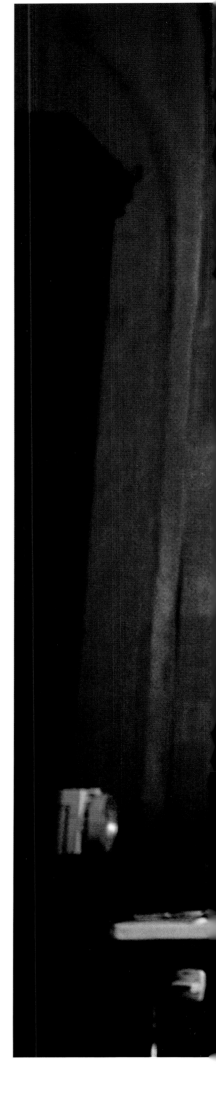

Paddy Gleeson of O'Callaghan's-Mills,
Co Clare, celebrates his 100th birthday
in May 2004 with the distinction of having
voted in every General Election since the
foundation of the State in 1922

Eamon Ward THE CLARE CHAMPION

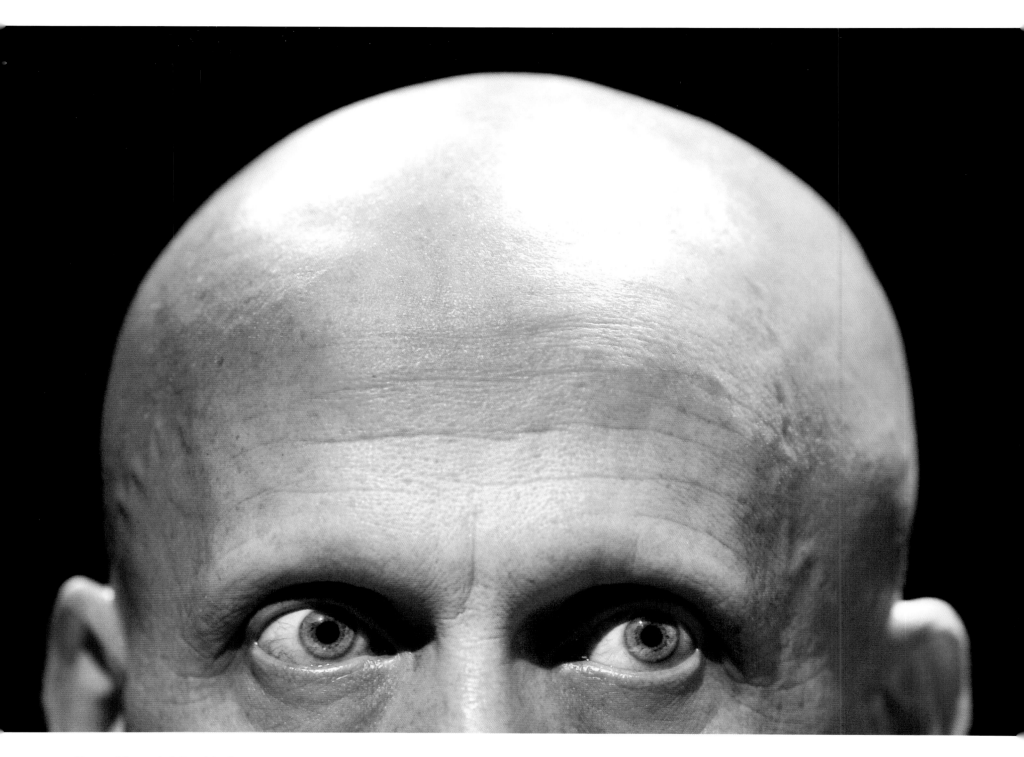

The world's most distinguished soccer
referee, Pierluigi Collina of Italy, answers
questions during a function in Dublin
City University in January 2004

Dara Mac Dónaill THE IRISH TIMES

The veteran broadcaster Gay Byrne stands beside his portrait, painted by John Kindness, at the National Gallery, Dublin, in December 2000

Cyril Byrne THE IRISH TIMES

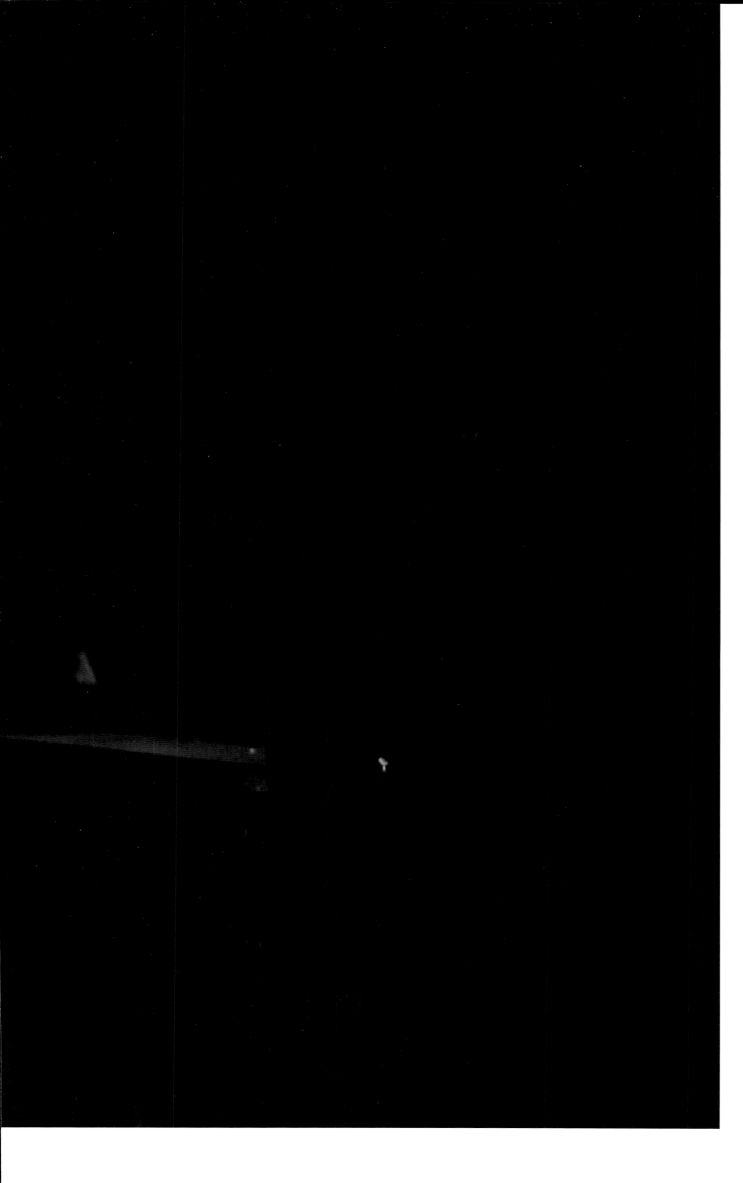

The entrepreneur and
racehorse breeder John
Magnier at the Curragh
in October 2005

Morgan Treacy
INPHO PHOTOGRAPHY

The Dublin Gaelic footballer Alan
Brogan at the Wellington monument in
Dublin's Phoenix Park in March 2006

Morgan Treacy INPHO PHOTOGRAPHY

Phillip Purdue of Clontarf Rugby
Club on a wet and muddy day in
the All-Ireland League in 2006

Morgan Treacy INPHO PHOTOGRAPHY

The Olympic swimmer
Chantal Gibney at the
Forty Foot, Sandycove,
Co Dublin, in June 2000

Billy Stickland
INPHO PHOTOGRAPHY

An Offaly hurler attempts to lift the ball from a waterlogged pitch during a Leinster Championship match in O'Moore Park, Portlaoise, in May 2006

Brendan Moran SPORTSFILE

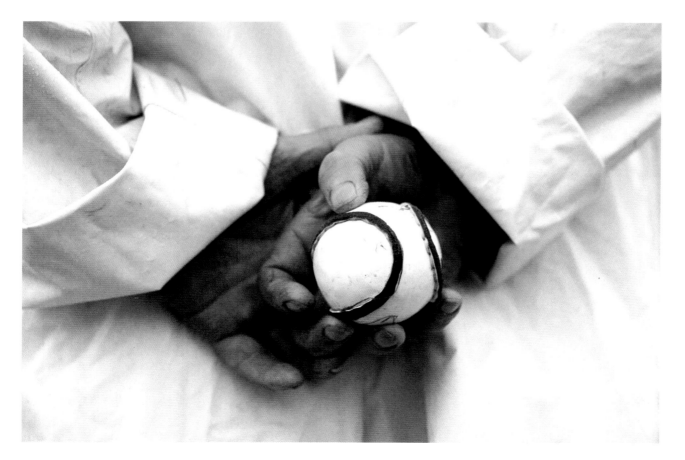

An umpire holds a sliotar during a championship hurling game at Casement Park, Belfast, in July 1999

David Maher SPORTSFILE

Josephat Kipkoviv of Kenya on his way to winning the 5,000-metre final during the Special Olympics World Summer Games at Dublin's Morton Stadium in June 2003

Ray McManus SPORTSFILE

The Olympic swimmer Nick O'Hare during a training session in March 1998

Matt Browne SPORTSFILE

Ireland's Sonia O'Sullivan shows her
delight on winning the 10,000-metre
final at the European Athletics
Championships in the Nepstadion,
Budapest, in August 1998

Brendan Moran SPORTSFILE

Sonia O'Sullivan, having been
lapped by all the other runners,
struggles to the finish of the
5,000-metre final at the Athens
Olympic Games in August 2004

Patrick Bolger
INPHO PHOTOGRAPHY

Meadhbh McGann from Laytown
offers encouragement to riders and
horses at Laytown Strand races,
Co Meath, in September 2006

Cyril Byrne THE IRISH TIMES

Nicky English, manager of the Tipperary hurling team, gives a leap of delight after his team beat Clare in the Munster Championship at Páirc Uí Chaoimh, Cork, in June 2001

Brendan Moran SPORTSFILE

A streaker is tackled by a policeman
during a rugby match between
Manawatu and the British and
Irish Lions in Palmerston North,
New Zealand, in June 2005

Billy Stickland INPHO PHOTOGRAPHY

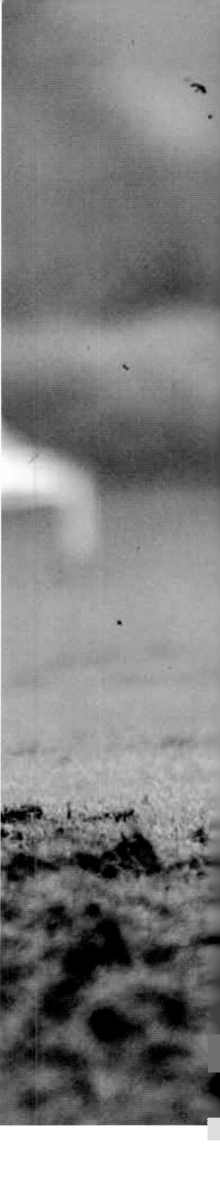

A hare tries to leap to freedom from
two greyhounds during the Irish
Coursing Cup finals at Ballybeggan,
Tralee, Co Kerry, in February 2002

Domnick Walsh EYE FOCUS

Joe Kernan, manager of the Armagh Gaelic
football team, celebrates after the All-
Ireland final at Croke Park in September
2002, his team having beaten Kerry to
win an historic first title for the county

Frank Miller THE IRISH TIMES

Clare footballers, mentors and fans celebrate at the end of the Munster Championship final at the Gaelic Grounds, Limerick, in July 1992, their team having achieved a rare victory over the perennial champions Kerry

Eamon Ward FREELANCE

Ireland's Girvan Dempsey dives for the line to score a try during the 16-7 defeat of Argentina at Lansdowne Road, Dublin, in November 2002

Eric Luke THE IRISH TIMES

Players pile up in the mud during
the rugby tour of South Africa by the
British and Irish Lions in June 1997

Billy Stickland INPHO PHOTOGRAPHY

Kilkenny players celebrate after beating
Cork in the final of the All-Ireland
Minor Camogie Championship at Croke
Park, Dublin, in September 2002

Bryan O'Brien THE IRISH TIMES

A bather on his way to the beach in Limassol watches two Republic of Ireland soccer fans pose for a photograph ahead of the Euro 2008 Championship qualifier against Cyprus in October 2006

Brian Lawless SPORTSFILE

Participants pay close attention as distances
from the jack get measured during a
bowls match between Shankill, Dublin,
and Shankill, Belfast, in April 2000

Cyril Byrne THE IRISH TIMES

Limerick hurling fans on the terrace at
Páirc Uí Chaoimh, Cork, during their team's
victory over Waterford in the Munster
Championship semi-final in June 2001

Eric Luke THE IRISH TIMES

The Republic of Ireland soccer captain
Andy Townsend samples the rudimentary
accommodation at Qemal Stafa stadium,
Tirana, before leading his team to a
2-1 victory against Albania in a World
Cup qualifying match in May 1993

Billy Stickland INPHO PHOTOGRAPHY

Republic of Ireland fans in the Maksimir Stadium, Zagreb, react to their team's defeat by Croatia in a European Championship qualifier in September 1999

David Maher SPORTSFILE

The Republic of Ireland player Roy Keane and manager Mick McCarthy at arm's length after a game in Lansdowne Road in September 2001; their differences would come to a head in Saipan the following year

Lorraine O'Sullivan

INPHO PHOTOGRAPHY

Building workers in Dublin city look through a hole cut in a promotional picture of Roy Keane the day after the announcement he was leaving Ireland's World Cup squad in Saipan following a row with the manager Mick McCarthy in May 2002

Bryan O'Brien THE IRISH TIMES

The Republic of Ireland soccer manager
Mick McCarthy is the focus of attention at
Lansdowne Road during his first game
in charge, against Russia in March 1996

Billy Stickland INPHO PHOTOGRAPHY

The scorekeeper Flan McNamara
keeps tabs on the action during
a hurling match at Cusack
Park, Ennis, in January 2007

Eamon Ward
FREELANCE / THE CLARE PEOPLE

A ticketless Spanish fan and an
official inside the gate fail to see eye
to eye on the occasion of a soccer
match between Shelbourne and
Deportivo de La Coruña at Lansdowne
Road, Dublin, in August 2004

Maura Hickey FREELANCE

All is relative calm outside Pearse Park,
Longford, before a Leinster Championship
match between the footballers of
Longford and Dublin in June 2006

Ray McManus SPORTSFILE

The Dublin footballers Senan Connell and Tom Mulligan celebrate in front of fans on Hill 16 after victory over Kildare in the Leinster Championship at Croke Park in July 2002

Frank Miller THE IRISH TIMES

Pat Roe of Laois and Tommy Dowd of Meath tussle during a Leinster Football Championship game at Páirc Tailteann, Navan, in June 1994

Dara Mac Dónaill IRISH INDEPENDENT

Brian O'Driscoll scores a try for Leinster in their Celtic League game against Munster at Lansdowne Road in October 2006

Billy Stickland INPHO PHOTOGRAPHY

Italy's Christian Vieri shoots at the Republic of Ireland goal during a friendly match at Lansdowne Road in August 2005

Brian Lawless SPORTSFILE

Galway's Alan Kerins keeps his eyes on the sliotar despite the challenge from Tipperary's Hugh Moloney during an All-Ireland hurling quarter-final at Croke Park, Dublin, in July 2005

Brendan Moran SPORTSFILE

The referee Aodán Mac Suibhne tries to separate Kilkenny's John Hoyne and Cork's Ronan Curran during the All-Ireland hurling final at Croke Park in September 2004

Alan Betson THE IRISH TIMES

Jack O'Connor, the Kerry team manager,
walks home through the rain in September
2004 with the most coveted trophy
in Irish sport, the Sam Maguire Cup for
Gaelic football's All-Ireland winners

Michelle Cooper-Galvin FREELANCE

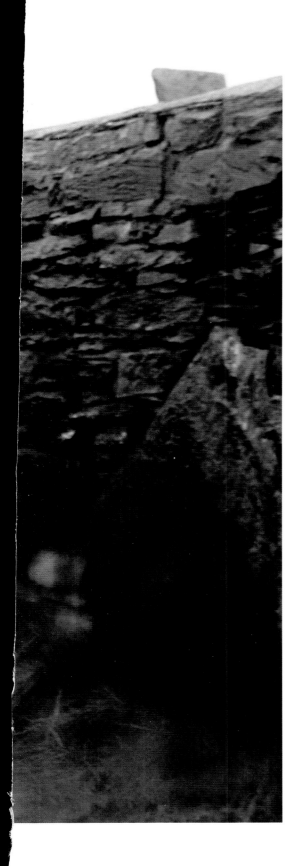

The Sam Maguire Cup on tour in Donegal after
the county won the All-Ireland Senior Football
Championship for the first time in September 1992

Billy Stickland INPHO PHOTOGRAPHY

Kilkenny players celebrate after
beating Carlow in the final of the
Leinster Minor Hurling Championship
at Croke Park in July 2006

Andrew Paton INPHO PHOTOGRAPHY

A groundsman re-marks the pitch during heavy rain
to allow a League of Ireland soccer match to proceed
at Dublin's Dalymount Park in October 2000

David Maher SPORTSFILE

A competitor runs his own race at the rear
of the field during the Clare Community
Games finals in Ennis in June 1999

John C Kelly THE CLARE CHAMPION

The rider James Redpath finds a soft landing
on hay bales when thrown from his machine
during the National Road Racing Championships
at Athea, Co Limerick, in June 2005

Michael O'Neill ALLPIX / THE IRISH DAILY STAR

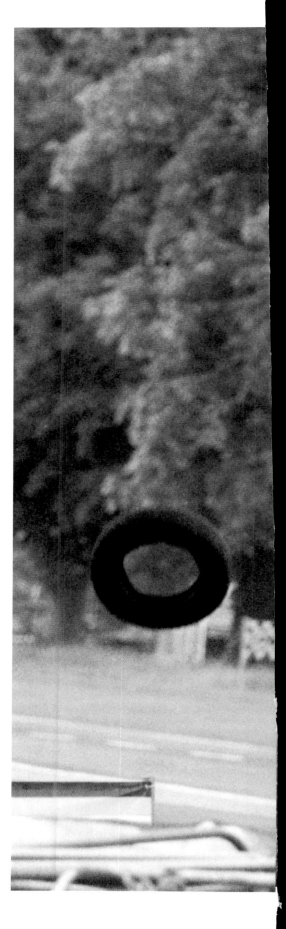

John Thomas McNamara and
Gee Dee crash to earth during the
County Clare Hunt Point-to-Point
at Dromoland in April 2006

John C Kelly THE CLARE CHAMPION

A Formula Vee car, with ts driver still
aboard, breaks up on impact during
the anrual motor races in Dublin's
Phoenix Park in September 1997

David Sleator THE IRISH TIMES

A woman watches the annual
races on Laytown Strand,
Co Meath, in September 2006

Patrick Bolger FREELANCE

A kilted piper watches the annual
Dublin City Marathon in October 2002

Julien Behal MAXWELL PHOTOGRAPHY

A lone spectator watches as riders in the annual round-Ireland Milk Rás flash past on the way to Cahersiveen, Co Kerry, in May 2004

Lorraine O'Sullivan INPHO PHOTOGRAPHY

The peloton in the annual round-Ireland Milk Rás stretches out on the way up to Moll's Gap, Co Kerry, in May 2001

Lorraine O'Sullivan
INPHO PHOTOGRAPHY

Teams weigh in (facing page) and take to the field to compete in intercounty tug-of-war contests in Carlow in 2001

Lar Boland FREELANCE

Shells are ejected from a shotgun at the Courtlough shooting ground, Balbriggan, Co Dublin, in May 2005

David Sleator THE IRISH TIMES

Racing pigeons take to the air at
Tramore, Co Waterford, in 2002 for
the flight back to Northern Ireland

Lar Boland FREELANCE

A greyhound is weighed in
preparation for a race at Dublin's
Shelbourne Park in 1994

Lar Boland FREELANCE

Young jockeys ride in a flapper race at Athea, Co Limerick, in August 2004

Brendan Landy FREELANCE

Bookmakers watch a race
during a point-to-point
meeting at Tinahely,
Co Wicklow, in 2002

Lar Boland FREELANCE

Contestants in the 'best-dressed lady' competition line up during the Irish Derby meeting at The Curragh, Co Kildare, in June 2004

Marc O'Sullivan FREELANCE

Limerick hurlers take to the field for the start of their National League game against Offaly at O'Connor Park, Tullamore, in March 2008

David Maher SPORTSFILE